Plants

Leaves

Patricia Whitehouse

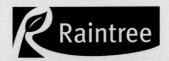
Raintree

www.raintreepublishers.co.uk
Visit our website to find out more information about **Raintree** books.

To order:
☎ Phone 44 (0) 1865 888112
▤ Send a fax to 44 (0) 1865 314091
▢ Visit the Raintree Bookshop at **www.raintreepublishers.co.uk** to browse our catalogue and order online.

First published in Great Britain by Raintree,
Halley Court, Jordan Hill, Oxford OX2 8EJ,
part of Harcourt Education.
Raintree is a registered trademark of Harcourt
Education Ltd.

Editorial: Nick Hunter and Diyan Leake
Design: Sue Emerson (HL-US) and Joanna Sapwell
(www.tipani.co.uk)
Picture Research: Amor Montes de Oca (HL-US)
Production: Jonathan Smith

Originated by Dot Gradations
Printed and bound in China by South China
Printing Company

ISBN 1 844 21065 0
07 06 05 04 03
10 9 8 7 6 5 4 3 2 1

J575.57
1445885

British Library Cataloguing in Publication Data
Whitehouse, Patricia
Leaves
575.5'7
A full catalogue record for this book is available
from the British Library.

Acknowledgements
The publishers would like to thank the following
for permission to reproduce photographs:
Amor Montes de Oca pp. **16**, **18**, back cover
(lettuce); Color Pic, Inc. pp. **4**, **9**, **20** (Peter Gregg),
21, **22**, **23** (branch and bud, E. R. Degginger), **24**
(E. R. Degginger); Dwight Kuhn pp. **1**, **15**, **23**
(stem); Eileen R. Herrling pp. **19**, **23** (roof); Jack
Glisson p. **10**; Lynn M. Stone p. **6**; Perkins/
Magnum/PictureQuest p. **11** (Chris Steele); Richard
Shiell p. **12**; Visuals Unlimited pp. **5** (Gary W.
Cater), **7** (Gerald Van Dyke), **14** (Wally Eberhart),
23 (vine, Gary W. Carter); Willard Clay
Photography, Inc. pp. **13** (Joseph Kayne), **17**.

Cover photograph of leave reproduced with
permission of Amor Montes de Oca.

Every effort has been made to contact copyright
holders of any material reproduced in this book.
Any omissions will be rectified in subsequent
printings if notice is given to the publishers.

Some words are shown in bold, **like this.** You can find them in the glossary on page 23.

Contents

What are leaves? 4

Why do plants have leaves? 6

Where do leaves come from? 8

What size do leaves come in? 10

How many leaves can plants have? 12

What shapes do leaves come in? 14

What colours are leaves? 16

How do people use leaves? 18

How do animals use leaves? 20

Quiz 22

Glossary 23

Index 24

Answers to quiz 24

What are leaves?

branch

Leaves are an important part of a plant.

They grow on the **branches** of trees.

stem

vine

Leaves grow on the **stems** of other plants.

Grape **vines** have big leaves.

Why do plants have leaves?

Leaves make food for plants.

They use water, air and sunlight to make the food.

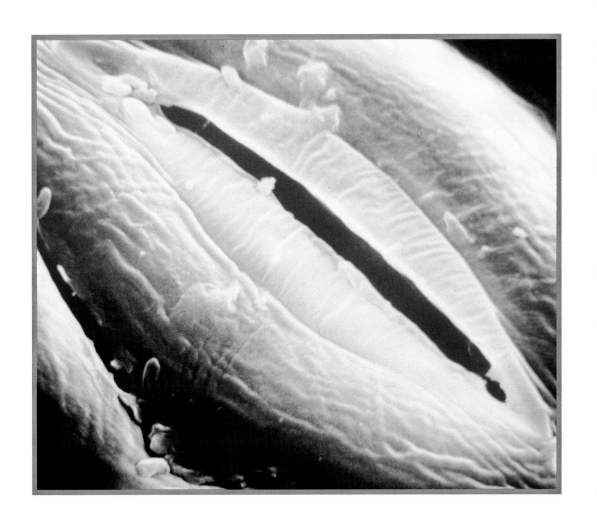

Leaves help plants breathe.

Holes in the leaves let air in and out.

Where do leaves come from?

seed

leaf

Leaves begin inside **seeds**.

You can see a tiny leaf inside this seed.

The seeds grow into plants.

Then new leaves grow inside **buds**.

What size do leaves come in?

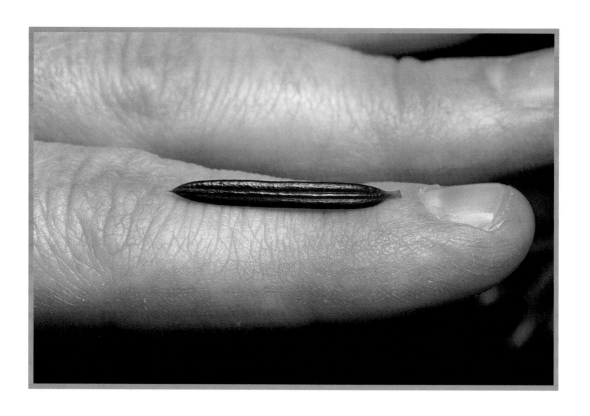

Leaves come in many sizes.

Some leaves can fit on your finger.

Some leaves are as big as
your hand.

Some leaves are almost as big
as you are!

How many leaves can plants have?

Some plants have just a few leaves.

This desert lily does not have many leaves.

Some plants have hundreds
of leaves.

Look at all the leaves on this
maple tree.

What shapes do leaves come in?

Leaves come in lots of different shapes.

They can be thin or round or have pointy edges.

All the leaves on one plant are the same shape.

What colours are leaves?

Most leaves are green, but they can be other colours.

They can be red or purple or have stripes or dots.

In some places, leaves change colour in the autumn.

Then, the leaves can be red or gold.

How do people use leaves?

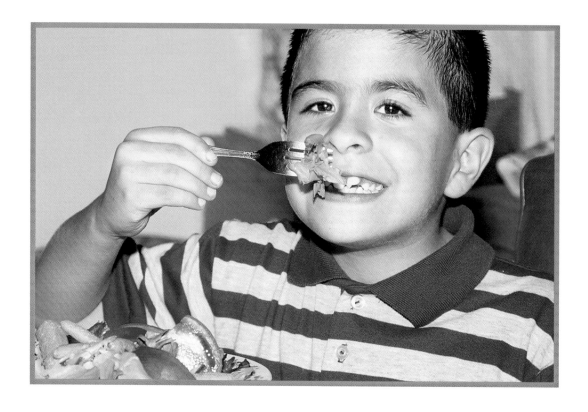

People use leaves for food.

When you eat lettuce, you are eating leaves.

roof

People use leaves to make things.

This **roof** is made of leaves.

How do animals use leaves?

Animals use leaves for food.

This rabbit is eating leaves.

Animals use leaves to build
their homes.

This squirrel nest is made of leaves.

Quiz

Do you remember what leaves do for plants?

Look for the answers on page 24.

Glossary

branch
part of a tree where the leaves grow

bud
flower or leaf that is still tightly closed

roof
part that covers the top of a house

stem
part of a plant where the buds, leaves and flowers grow

vine
plant that has a long climbing stem

Index

air   7

animals   20, 21

branches   4, 23

buds   9, 23

colours   16 –17

food   6, 18, 20

people   18, 19

seeds   8, 9

shapes   14, 15

sizes   10

stems   5, 23

trees   4, 13

vines   5, 23

Answers to quiz on page 22

Leaves make food for plants.

Leaves help plants breathe.

Titles in the Plants series include:

Hardback   1 844 21064 2

Hardback   1 844 21065 0

Hardback   1 844 21066 9

Hardback   1 844 21067 7

Hardback   1 844 21068 5

Hardback   1 844 21069 3

Find out about the other titles in this series on our website www.raintreepublishers.co.uk